# What's special to me?

# Religious Food

Anita Ganeri

**WAYLAND**

# Contents

**All Wayland books encourage children to read and help them improve their literacy.**

✓ The contents page, page numbers, headings and index help to locate a particular piece of information.

✓ The glossary reinforces alphabetic knowledge and extends vocabulary.

✓ The books to read section suggests other books dealing with the same subject.

# Special Food

What is your favourite thing to eat? Is it ice-cream, sweets or delicious pizza? Why do you like it so much?

In the world's religions, many special kinds of foods are eaten every day and at festival times. Each food has a special meaning. They help people to follow their faith and to learn more about it.

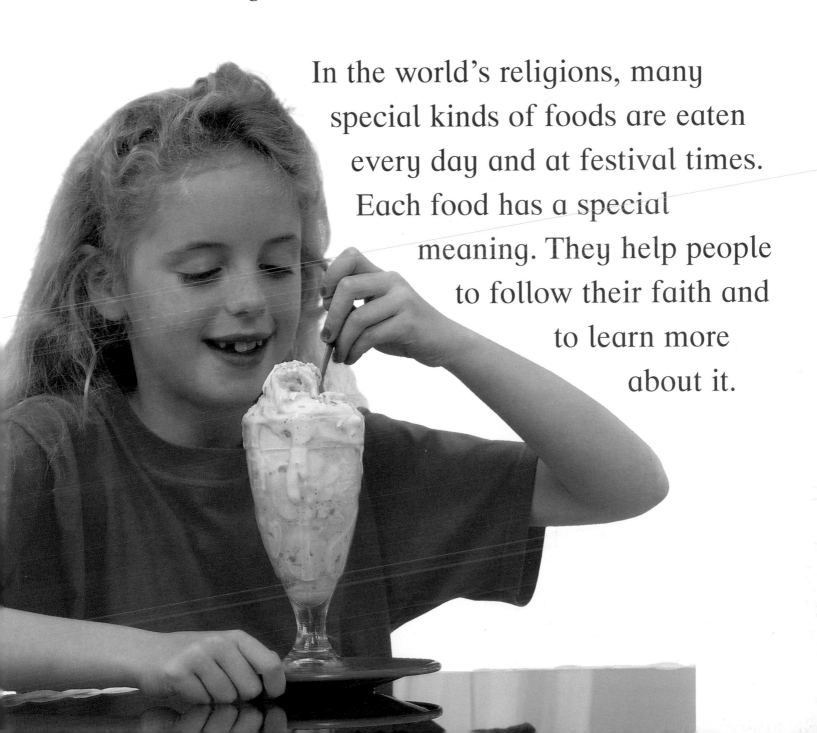

# Hindu Offerings

Many Hindus are vegetarians. They believe that all life is **holy**. They do not eat meat because they do not want to kill or harm any animals. Hindus eat their food with their fingers from large plates, called thalis, like the one below.

When Hindus worship, they offer food to God. This can be sweets or fruit, like coconuts or bananas. Offerings like these are called **prashad**. Everyone shares the food and receives God's **blessing**.

At a Hindu wedding, the bride and groom sprinkle roasted rice, butter and grain into a special fire. They believe that the fire carries their offerings up to God. Afterwards, there is a great feast.

Sweets are made at home or bought from sweet shops or stalls. At weddings and festivals, Hindus give gifts of sweets to friends and relations. The sweets are made from milk, nuts, coconut and sugar.

# Jewish Food Laws

On Friday night, a Jewish family eats a meal together to celebrate the start of Shabbat. This is the Jewish holy day. The meal begins with a blessing said over a glass of wine.

This is a loaf of challah which is specially baked bread for Shabbat. It is made in the shape of a plait. There are always two loaves of challah on the Shabbat table. Everyone in the family has a share.

There are many rules about Jewish food. Food which Jews may eat is called **kosher**. It can be bought from a kosher shop or stall. Kosher food includes fruit, vegetables, beef, lamb and fish. Pork, rabbit and shellfish are not kosher.

Each of the foods on this plate has a special meaning. The foods are eaten at the Jewish festival of **Pesach**, or Passover. They remind people how, long ago, God helped the Jews to escape from Egypt.

# Buddhist Food Gifts

Buddhist monks are given food by followers who live near their monastery. This is called giving **alms**. Giving alms to the monks and nuns is part of a Buddhist's duty.

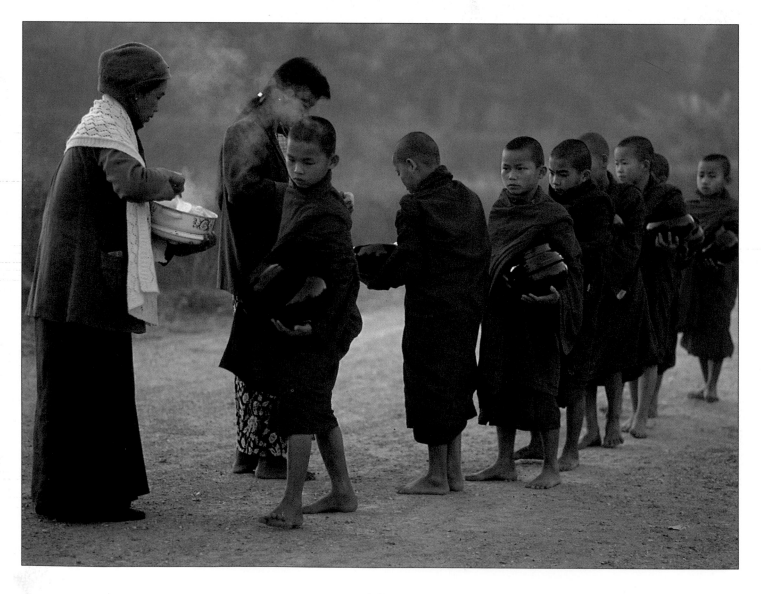

These monks are having their one meal of the day, which they always eat before midday. After this, they can drink water but will go without food until the next day.

On special occasions, such as the Buddha's birthday, people take food, flowers and **incense** to the monastery. These are offered to a buddharupa, a statue of the Buddha. Then the food is given to the monks as a gift.

At festival times, Buddhists visit the monastery to honour the Buddha and to enjoy a meal together. Many Buddhists do not eat meat because they do not believe in killing or harming animals.

# Special Christian Food

At a service that is often called Holy Communion, Christians eat bread and drink wine which has been blessed by a priest or minister. This reminds Christians of the last meal that Jesus ate with his friends. It helps them to feel closer to him.

This boy is making pancakes to celebrate Shrove Tuesday. This is the day before Lent. People use up the rich foods in their house, such as eggs, butter and oil. During Lent, many Christians give up eating some types of food. They remember how Jesus once spent forty days **fasting** in the wilderness.

At Easter, Christians eat hot cross buns to remind them of how Jesus died on the cross. Three days later, Jesus was resurrected, which means that he came back from the dead. Christians eat Easter eggs at Easter to celebrate new life.

This church is decorated with fruit, vegetables, bread and flowers to celebrate the harvest festival. Christians go to a service in church to say 'thank you' for the harvest and for all God's gifts and goodness.

# Muslim Fasts and Feasts

For Muslims, sharing food with guests is an important way of making them welcome. This picture shows Muslims eating a midday meal of chicken, rice and bread.

Food which Muslims are allowed to eat is called **halal**. Muslims can buy halal meat, fruit and vegetables at special shops like this one. Muslims are not allowed to eat pork or to drink alcohol.

 During **Ramadan**, Muslims fast from dawn to sunset. This means they have nothing to eat or drink. They do this to obey **Allah**'s wishes. After evening prayers, they enjoy a family meal.

These sweets and sugared almonds are for the festival of Id-ul-Fitr, which marks the end of Ramadan. This happy occasion begins with a great feast. People also exchange gifts and cards.

# Sikhs Sharing Food

At the end of all Sikh services, everyone shares a sweet pudding called karah prasad, eaten from the same dish. It is prepared in a special way. A prayer is said and a special sword called a **kirpan** is used to mix the ingredients together.

Here, karah prasad is being given out at the end of a Sikh wedding. Sikhs gain strength from eating and worshipping together. Sharing food also shows that everyone is equal in God's eyes.

The end of a service is usually followed by a shared meal in the **langar**. This is the name for the **gurdwara**'s kitchen and all the food cooked in it. The meal is served to all the worshippers and given free to all. Many people help to cook and serve it.

A special ceremony is held at which Sikhs become full members of their religion. They drink a mixture of sugar and water called amrit. It is stirred with a double-edged sword called a **khanda**. Amrit is also sprinkled on their heads and hands.

# Notes for teachers

**Pages 4 &5** A Hindu meal traditionally consists of several different vegetable dishes, together with rice or bread, such as chappatis. It is served in small, separate dishes on a large steel tray called a thali, or on a banana leaf. Most Hindus are vegetarians, although some eat chicken and fish. Hindus do not eat beef because they believe that the cow is sacred. This is because it is linked to the god Krishna, who was brought up by a cowherd and his wife, and because it provides life-sustaining milk and dung for fuel. As part of their culture, Hindus eat with their right hands. The left hand is traditionally associated with 'unclean' tasks, such as washing. Prashad is food which is offered to God in a temple or home shrine to be blessed. It is then shared out among the worshippers so that everyone shares in God's blessing.

**Pages 6 &7** Food plays an important part in a Hindu wedding. It is used symbolically during the religious ceremony, conducted by a priest around the sacred fire. Apart from sprinkling rice, grains and ghee (clarified butter) into the sacred fire, the couple shower each other with rice grains which have been blessed by the priest. Hindu weddings can be very lavish. After the religious ceremony, there is a sumptuous feast for the guests. As at all Hindu celebrations and festivals, gift boxes of Indian sweets are sent to friends, relatives and business associates to mark the happy occasion. Each region of India has its own speciality sweets.

**Pages 8 & 9** On Shabbat, the evening family meal begins with a blessing said over the wine and the two loaves of challah. This is then shared out among all those present. There are always two loaves of bread on the table in memory of the time that the Jews spent wandering in the wilderness after the Exodus from Egypt. They had to collect two portions of manna, (the food sent to them by God), on the day before Shabbat. This is because Shabbat was a day of rest so no baking could be done. The challah is covered with a cloth embroidered with Shabbat symbols such as the plaited challah loaves themselves, a bottle of wine or the Shabbat candles.

**Pages 10 &11** The laws governing what Jews may or may not eat are set out in the Torah, part of the Jewish scripture. Many Jews keep these laws very strictly. All fruit and vegetables may be eaten. Animals with cloven hooves

which chew the cud, such as sheep, goats, cows and deer are kosher but animals that are only one of these things, such as pigs or camels, are not. Most birds are not kosher, apart from ducks, chickens and turkeys. Fish are only kosher if they have fins and scales. Shellfish are not permitted. Dairy foods, such as milk and butter, are not eaten at the same time as meat. The foods served at Pesach are part of the ceremony called the Seder. They remind Jews of their ancestors' slavery in Egypt and of their escape. A lamb bone is a reminder of the lambs killed in Egypt; an egg of the offerings made to God; a piece of lettuce or parsley is a sign of spring and of hope for the future; bitter horseradish represents the Jews' unhappiness; a sweet paste of apples, wine and nuts, called charoset, stands for the mortar which the Jews used to make buildings for the Egyptian king. A bowl of salty water stands for tears. There is also a plate of flat crackers called matzot.

**Pages 12 & 13, 14 & 15** For Buddhists, a gift or an act of generosity towards a monk or nun is called dana. It is believed to bring the givers merit which will help them in their next lives (Buddhists believe in reincarnation). The most usual gift is that of the midday meal placed in the monks' alms bowls. Also listed in the sacred texts are clothing, means of transport, garlands, perfumes, ointment, bedding, dwellings and lighting. Apart from the gifts they receive from devotees, the monks and nuns own very few belongings. When offerings are made in the temple or monastery, food is placed in front of an image of the Buddha as an act of generosity. In Britain, many temples also have a kitchen where volunteers prepare food for the monks, devotees and other visitors, especially on special days, such as the Buddha's birthday.

**Pages 16 &17** Holy Communion, at which worshippers share bread and wine, is an important service in the Christian Church. The service is known by many different names e.g. Mass, the Eucharist, the Lord's Supper. It reminds Christians of Jesus's words to his disciples as they shared the Last Supper together. He told them that, whenever they ate bread or drank wine in the future, they should do so in memory of him. Ordinary bread is sometimes used but more often there are special round wafers marked with a cross. The bread is consecrated as the 'body' of Christ. The wine is consecrated as the 'blood' of

Christ. Lent is the name for the six weeks before Easter, beginning on Shrove Tuesday. It is when Christians remember the time Jesus spent in the wilderness. 'Shrove' means 'forgiven'. It is also a time for confessing any wrong doings in order to make a new start at Lent. Traditionally, plain food was eaten during Lent. Pancakes were made to use up any rich food in the house.

**Pages 18 & 19** It is traditional to eat hot cross buns on Good Friday, the day that Jesus was crucified. The cross is a reminder of how Jesus died. The mixture of spices in the dough reminds Christians of the spices which Mary Magdalene and a friend, who visited Jesus's tomb on the Sunday took to anoint his body. They found the tomb empty. Eggs are an ancient symbol of new life. Chocolate eggs are given at Easter to celebrate Jesus's new life when he rose again from the dead. The breaking of the egg may also suggest the opening of Jesus's empty tomb.

**Pages 20 & 21** In Islam, food which is allowed by Allah is called halal. Food which is forbidden by Allah is called haram. These rules are set down in the Qur'an, the Muslims' holy book. By obeying them, Muslims are obeying Allah's wishes for how they should live their lives. All fruit, vegetables and fish are halal. Meat, such as lamb, chicken and beef, is halal but only if it has been killed in a particular way. First, the animal must be dedicated to Allah. Then the animal's throat is cut and its blood is allowed to flow freely. It becomes unconscious immediately. Muslims are not allowed to eat pork nor anything that comes from a pig. Anything cooked with the fat of animals which have been sacrificed to Allah is also haram. Drinking alcohol is forbidden.

**Pages 22 & 23** During the month of Ramadan, Muslims fast from dawn until sunset. This is sawm, one of the Five Pillars of Islam. The purpose of fasting is to obey Allah's wishes, as set out in the Qur'an, and to practise both mental and physical self-discipline and self-control. It also helps Muslims to appreciate what it feels like to go hungry. All adult Muslims are obliged to fast. Children under seven do not fast and older children fast, but not as strictly as adults. People who are ill or physically weak are excused from fasting, as are menstruating or pregnant women. These people are expected to fast at a later date. Tables are published giving the times of sunrise and sunset during Ramadan so that people know when to begin their fast. At sunset, they have a light snack, followed by a main meal after evening prayers.

**Pages 24 & 25 & 26** Karah prasad is a sweet, pudding-like food made from flour, sugar, water and ghee (clarified butter). It is kept in a steel bowl and shared out at the end of all Sikh services and ceremonies. It is food that has been blessed by God and is shared out to show that, in God's eyes, everyone is equal. This is a key Sikh belief. The karah prasad is prepared in accordance with the Rahit Maryada, the Sikh code of behaviour, by men or women who have bathed and put on clean clothes. As they cook the mixture, they recite verses from the Guru Granth Sahib, the Sikh holy book. During worship it is placed near the Guru Granth Sahib in the gurdwara. The langar is a communal meal offered to all worshippers and visitors to the gurdwara. The practice was begun by Guru Nanak, the founder of Sikhism. The food is simple and vegetarian. Again, eating the langar together demonstrates that everyone is equal.

**Page 27** Amrit is a sweet water made by dissolving patases or sugar crystals. It is stirred in a steel bowl using a ceremonial double edged sword called a khanda. When babies are taken to the gurdwara to be named, they are sometimes given amrit afterwards. It is also drunk by Sikhs joining the Khalsa, the Sikh community, and becoming full members of their religion. Once again, it is drunk from a shared bowl to show equality. It is also sprinkled on the initiates' eyes and hair. The Khalsa was begun by Guru Gobind Singh in 1699.

# Glossary

**Allah** The Muslim name for God.

**alms** Gifts of money, food or clothes.

**blessing** God's love and care. A blessing is also a short prayer thanking or praising God.

**fasting** Going without food.

**gurdwara** A place where Sikh meet for worship and to learn.

**halal** Food which Muslims are allowed to eat.

**holy** To do with God or the gods. It also means someone or something that should be worshipped.

**incense** Sweet-smelling spices made into a block or stick.

**khanda** The sword that symbolizes the Sikh religion.

**kirpan** A steel dagger or sword worn by Sikhs, often as a smaller version, and used in Sikh ceremonies.

**kosher** Food which Jewish people are allowed to eat.

**langar** This means 'the anchor' and is a kitchen where the food is prepared.

**Pesach** A Jewish festival which celebrates how the Jews escaped from Egypt thousands of years ago. It is also called Passover.

**prashad** Food offered to God by Hindus as part of worship.

**Ramadan** A month in the Muslim calendar when Muslims fast from dawn until sunset.

# Books to read

HINDU
**Diwali** by Kerena Marchant (Wayland, 1996)
**Hindu** by Jenny Wood (Franklin Watts, 1996)

JEWISH
**The Seventh Day is Shabbat** by Margaret Barratt (Heinemann, 1994)
**Passover** by Angela Wood (Wayland, 1997)

BUDDHIST
**The Buddha's Birthday** by Margaret Barratt (Heinemann, 1994)
**My Buddhist Life** by Meg St. Pierre and Marty Casey (Wayland, 1996)

CHRISTIAN
**Bible Stories: Water into Wine** (Heinemann, 1998)
**Easter** by Philip Sauvain (Wayland, 1997)

**Lucy's Sunday** by Margaret Barratt (Heinemann, 1994)

SIKH
**I am a Sikh** by Manju Aggarwal (Franklin Watts, 1984)
**My Sikh Life** by Kanwaljit Kaur-Singh (Wayland, 1997)

**General series on religion:**
**Beliefs and Cultures** series (Franklin Watts, 1997/8)

**Everyday Religion** series (Wayland, 1996/7)

**Introducing Religions** series (Heinemann, 1997

**Looking at Christianity** and **Looking at Judaism** series (Wayland, 1998)

Editor: Sarah Doughty
Design: Sterling Associates
Consultant: Alison Seaman

First published in 1998 by
Wayland Publishers Ltd
61 Western Road, Hove
East Sussex, BN3 1JD

© Copyright 1998 Wayland Publishers Ltd

**Find Wayland on the Internet at http:/www.wayland.co.uk**

British Library Cataloguing in Publication Data
Ganeri, Anita
   Religious Food. – (What's Special to me?)
   1. Food – Religious aspects – Juvenile literature
   I. Title
   291.3'8

ISBN 0 7502 2244 1

Printed and bound by G.Canale & C.S.p.A., Turin

Picture Acknowledgements: Cephas (J. F. Riviere) 18, (Frank B. Higham) 19, (Nigel Blythe) 20; CIRCA Picture Library (John Smith) 25; Eye Ubiquitous (David Cumming) 6, (Paul Seheult) 18; Chris Fairclough 21, 27; Sally and Richard Greenhill (Sam Greenhill) 4; Robert Harding 8, 10, 11, 14; The Hutchison Library title page, 13, 16; Christine Osborne Pictures 4, 7, 9, 26; Panos Pictures (J. Holmes) 5, (Jean Leo Dugast) 12; Peter Sanders 22, 23; Trip (H Rogers) 15, (H Rogers) 24; Wayland Picture Library 3, 17.

# Index

Entries in **bold** are pictures